For Noirín and Julie

~ DARA

For Maisey

~ BARRY

DARA McANULTY

WILD CHILD

A JOURNEY THROUGH NATURE

ILLUSTRATED BY

BARRY FALLS

MACMILLAN CHILDREN'S BOOKS

First published 2021 by Macmillan Children's Books
an imprint of Pan Macmillan
The Smithson, 6 Briset Street, London EC1M 5NR
EU representative: Macmillan Publishers Ireland Limited,
Mallard Lodge, Lansdowne Village, Dublin 4
Associated companies throughout the world
www.panmacmillan.com

ISBN 978-1-5290-4532-1

Text copyright © Dara McAnulty 2021
Illustrations copyright © Barry Falls 2021

The right of Dara McAnulty and Barry Falls to be identified as the
author and illustrator of this work has been asserted by them in accordance
with the Copyright, Designs and Patents Act 1988.

Pan Macmillan does not have any control over, or any responsibility for,
any author or third-party websites referred to in or on this book.

1 3 5 7 9 8 6 4 2

A CIP catalogue record for this book is available from the British Library.

Design by Janene Spencer

Printed and bound in China

CONTENTS

I see you.

I see your eyes sparkle when you see shapes, watch flickers of light, buzzing and fluttering. I see you when you want to pick up that feather. That pebble. That leaf. Do you yearn to climb an oak tree, to get a bird's eye view of the world, to feel the wind of leaves?

Can I hold your hand? Can I show you the magic of nature?

Let me take you on a journey. A wild wandering. A fascinating world awaits.

At first you won't have to go far. You can watch from your window . . . you can discover your garden. Once you feel the tickle of excitement, you'll want to go further, and further.

Always remember to be gentle, that you are a protector of nature, you are a guardian and a seeker.

Can I take you on a journey?

Your friend, a friend of nature,

Dara

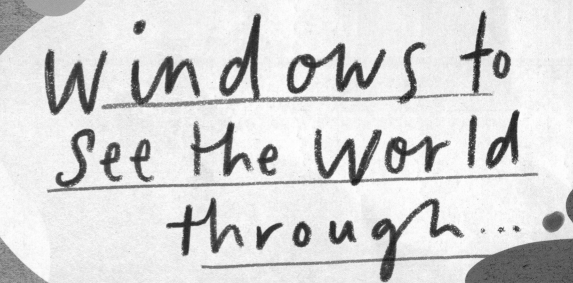

1
windows to see the world through...

Let me give you new windows to see the world through. Flashes of colour will become clear.

You will see every detail, every delicate shade, every movement. Here, let me help you. It may be raining but we can still see.

Let's bring a chair to the window, let me grow you.

What can you see?

Springing forward, scuttling, a bird as black as night.
Bright orange beak, amber light. Glossy silken feathers,
rapid twitching wings. Suddenly, still, to pierce soft earth.
A wriggling mass pecked out, flight to branch into leaves.

Acrobat is twirling, birdfeeder as branch. Tiny claws clinging,
clenched to swing and feast on seed. Shiny black cap,
snow-white cheeks, steely-grey back flits and twists.
Mesmerising movement to and fro, pendulum bird.

There is a tremble in the leaves, a whizzing ball of light.
A moment of rest reveals brown feathers speckled white.
Tail held high, like a wizard flicking a wand, moving like
musical notes do, undulating flight. Disappearing act.

Alighting from the sky like fire. A twitching crown of ruby,
pearl and darkest black. Wings like restless twitching fans, gilded
with glistening gold. Like an artist painted their feathers.

 Mum! I need to go outside, now!

I don't care if it's raining, I don't care if it's wet.
I want to see it all now, come on, I just can't wait!

As soon as you go out, though, the birds will fly away,
but I know other creatures and where they like to stay.

A male **BLACKBIRD** has black feathers and an orange beak. The female looks very different, she has brown feathers and a brown beak. A cool scientific name for this is dimorphism. Blackbirds love to sing after the rain has stopped and they have one of the most beautiful songs of all the garden birds.

The blackbirds are home birds and stay close to where they hatched. The oldest one recorded was twenty years old!

Male blackbird

Coal Tit

COAL TITS are acrobats and love to swing upside down using strong flexible legs to grip almost anything. From washing line to bird feeder and sometimes even the edge of a gutter. As their little bodies are unable to store food as reserves of fat, they hide their seeds in secret spots under autumn leaves. They do this so the coal tits can eat it later in the wintertime when all the food is gone.

A group of coal tits is called a banditry. They nest in the holes in trees, but they will use a nest box. Sometimes gangs of these bandits will clear a bird feeder in a short period of time before the bigger birds arrive and bully them away.

size comparison

Wren

WRENS sometimes form communal roosts in winter, huddling up like emperor penguins. The record is sixty-three wrens in one bird box. This is done so they can share body heat, which is very important because they are so tiny, and winters can be freezing.

The wrens have a melodious, high-pitched but very loud song which always catches people off guard.

The males make more than one nest using moss, leaves and grass. This is so the female can choose which nest she likes best.

Goldfinch

GOLDFINCH males have slightly longer beaks than females so they can reach teasel seeds.

A group of goldfinches is called a charm. To lure a goldfinch into your garden, put out some Nyjer seed, which is one of their favourite foods.

Young goldfinches do not have the ruby crown of the adults.

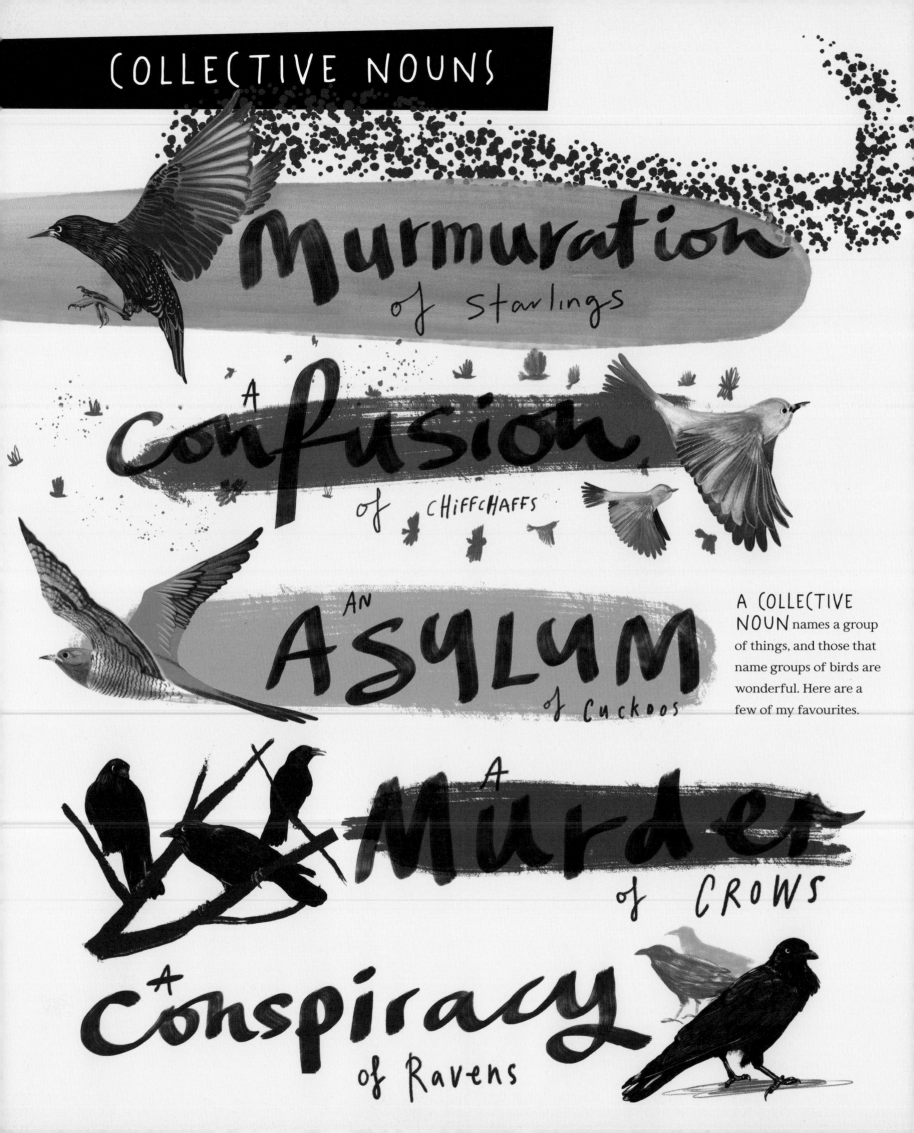

COLLECTIVE NOUNS

Murmuration of Starlings

A **confusion** of CHIFFCHAFFS

An **ASYLUM** of Cuckoos

A COLLECTIVE NOUN names a group of things, and those that name groups of birds are wonderful. Here are a few of my favourites.

A **Murder** of CROWS

A **Conspiracy** of Ravens

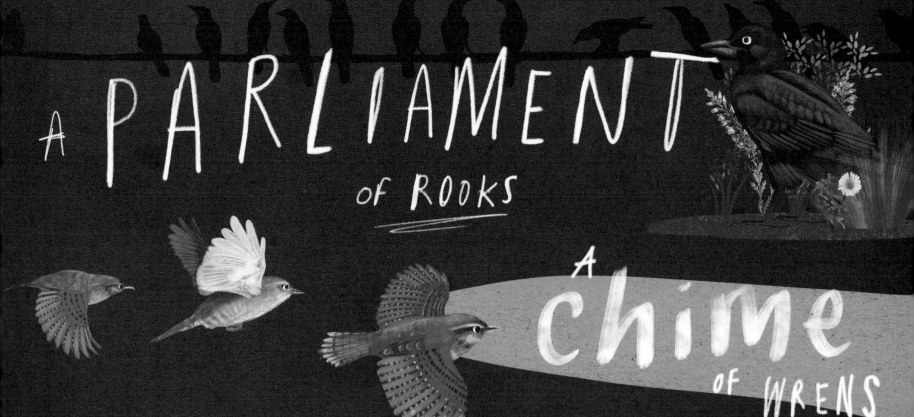

A **PARLIAMENT** OF ROOKS

A **chime** OF WRENS

A **Quarrel** OF SPARROWS

A **BOOBY** OF NUTHATCHES

A **BANDITRY** OF COALTITS

A **CHARM** OF GOLDFINCHES

MAKING A BIRD FEEDER

YOU WILL NEED:

A cardboard tube

Two long, thin sticks

Some lard

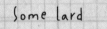

Birdseed, such as sunflower hearts

A butter knife or spatula

A piece of string for hanging up your bird feeder

1

Ask a grown-up to help you make four evenly spaced holes at one end of the tube. You will put the thin sticks through these to make a cross shape. This will give the birds somewhere to perch while they eat the seed.

2

Make two more holes, opposite each other, on the other end of the tube to put the string through to hang the feeder up.

3

Use the spatula to coat the tube with lard.

4

Roll the tube in the birdseed, which will stick to the lard.

5

Thread the sticks through the four holes (they should now be at the bottom of the tube).

6

Thread the piece of string through the two holes (it should be at the top) and hang the seed out on a bird feeder or branch for coal tits and goldfinches to enjoy.

2 The G

ARDEN

In the time it took us to get ready, the rain has gone away,
the sun is peeking out, beckoning an explorer's eye.
Have you got your magnifying glass? Are you ready for
a closer look? Let's uncover all the garden mysteries in
crannies and little nooks.

What can you find?

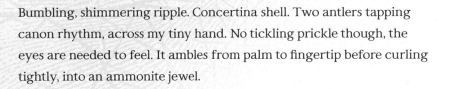

Bumbling, shimmering ripple. Concertina shell. Two antlers tapping
canon rhythm, across my tiny hand. No tickling prickle though, the
eyes are needed to feel. It ambles from palm to fingertip before curling
tightly, into an ammonite jewel.

Earth worker appears, wriggling, thick. A hundred pink rings.
Ploughman. Surging up with new rain, a curling tendril, soil-covered.
It does tickle. Squiggly, magic scent of weather and all that holds life
together. I feel its energy and bow my head with thankful smile.

A humming and thrumming is whizzing, zinging through the air.
A zooming of black and yellow buzzing. Landing on dazzling nectar
fuel. What is this yellow flower, opened like the sun? Another beside
with the same leaves but topped with feathery fluff. Under soft touch
of finger, seeds scatter, float, disperse. Triple flowers. Sun. Moon. Stars.

Crawling now, yearning to sink deep into grass. Thin green stems
reveals tiny, orange, EGG! Fluttering wings of mossy web, glorious
orange tips. Land on delicate purple petal, restless flickers fleeting visit.
Leaving bedazzled eyes, and delightful dizzy head. Touching the tiny
orange egg, heart feels a different kind of beat.

FACTS

Woodlice

WOODLICE have two antennae that they use to touch and feel the world. They also have two small tubes sticking out of the back of the body. Known as uropods, these help a woodlouse find its way, but some species release chemicals from them to deter predators. Woodlice belong to a big group of crustaceans, called isopods, and are related to crabs and lobsters. There are more than 10,400 species of isopod, living on every continent except Antarctica – including under the sea.

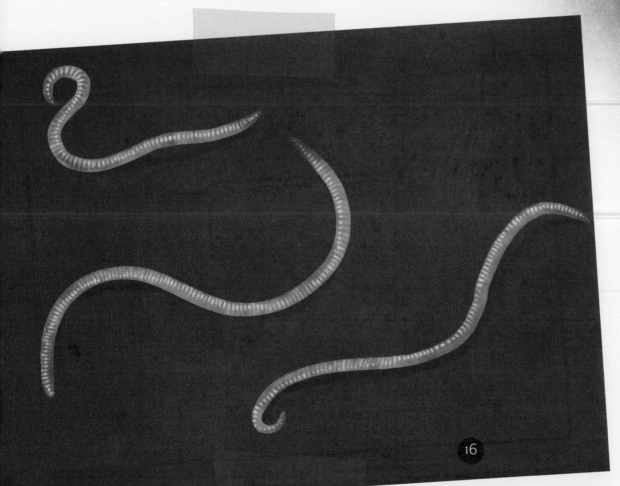

BUTCHY BOYS
PENNY SOW
Woodpig
CHEESELOG
Granny-greys
SLATERS
WITCH of THE ASHES
Chisel BOB
BOATBUILD
Chuggy-pegs
Monkey-peas

EARTHWORMS

In one acre of healthy soil there can live up to a million EARTHWORMS.

Earthworms are so interesting that the famous naturalist Charles Darwin studied them for thirty-nine years. The largest earthworm was found in South Africa and was six and a half metres long. They don't have any eyes but they can use their sensitive skin to 'see' sunlight and move away from it by burrowing into the damp, dark soil.

Bees & Dandelions

HONEYBEES communicate by dancing with each other.

BUMBLEBEES are really furry to protect them from the early spring cold. This means they can start flying earlier in the year to harvest food from dandelions.

The name **DANDELIONS** comes from the French 'dent de lion', which means a tooth of a lion, because the leaves are shaped like teeth. Dandelions are wildflowers that are much loved by many pollinator insects.

Cuckoo flower and ORANGE-TIP BUTTERFLY

The leaves of a **CUCKOO FLOWER** are edible and taste really peppery. Make sure there are no caterpillars or eggs on the leaf you are eating. In European legend the cuckoo flowers are sacred to fairies, so you mustn't take them inside.

ORANGE-TIP CATERPILLARS usually eat cuckoo flowers or garlic mustard. The caterpillar will actually eat any other orange-tip eggs it finds when it emerges from the pupa. This means it won't have to compete with a rival for food. To prevent this, the adult usually lays a single egg on each plant.

CLASSIFICATION

HOMO SAPIENS

Have you anything in common with anyone or do you share a characteristic with any animal or plant? You might have the same colour eyes or both have a skeleton, for example. Do you have a pet? What characteristics do you share with them? There are so many different animals and plants in the world that scientists ordered them into groups that share similar characteristics, such as number of legs or size and shape of flowers.

WHEN DID CLASSIFICATION BEGIN AND WHO STARTED IT ALL?

For thousands of years nature-lovers have collected animals and plants, named them and wondered how they were related to each other. Nearly 300 years ago a Swedish scientist, called Carl Linnaeus, decided to name different living things using a system that everyone around the world could understand. He hoped that the new names would also help scientists understand how different animals and plants were related to each other.

This is called classification, and nowadays it also tells us a great deal about how the story of life on Earth and organisms evolved.

The simplest arrangement Linnaeus made was species. He then grouped species into genus, family, order, class, phylum and kingdom. Domain was later added by modern scientists.

WHY DOES CLASSIFICATION USE LATIN?

During Linnaeus's time, most European scientists would have known the old Roman language Latin, and also Ancient Greek. Scientists used these languages to create the new names for Linnaeus's system of classification. They often wrote in Latin so they could easily share their findings with each other, even if they spoke different languages.

Today, Latin and Greek are still often used to create scientific names for organisms. Each type, or species, of organism is given a name with two parts, which is the system that Linnaeus suggested. The first part of the name is the genus and the second part is the species. Humans, for example, have the genus *Homo* (which means 'man') and our species is *sapiens* (which means 'wise'.)

If you have a cat as a pet, its scientific name is *Felis catus* and you both share the same characteristics that make you mammals!

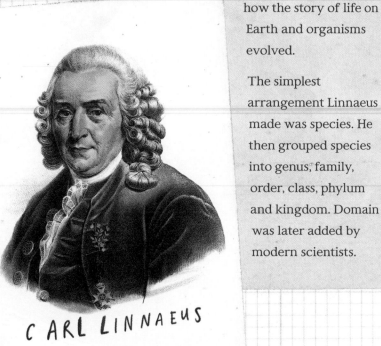

CARL LINNAEUS

CANIS LUPUS.

18

DOMAIN

KINGDOM

PHYLUM

CLASS

ORDER

FAMILY

GENUS

SPECIES

EUKARYA

ANIMALIA

CHORDATA

MAMMALIA

CARNIVORA

CANIDAE

VULPES

VULPES

RED FOX

EUKARYA

PLANTAE

ANTHOPHYTA

EUDICOTS

ROSALES

ROSACEAE

MALUS

DOMESTICA

APPLE

MAKING A
TERRARIUM

A glass jar with a lid of any size will do so long as you can fit a small plant in it

Moss

Pebbles

Sterile potting mix

Activated charcoal, which you can get from a garden centre

A small plant

A teaspoon/tweezers, or very small hands

20

1

Fill the bottom of the jar with pebbles as the first layer. This allows water to drain away from the soil and stay in the jar, so it evaporates to create a water cycle.

2

Next put some activated charcoal into the terrarium – this helps to keep the water fresh.

3

Now add a layer of moss to stop the soil from going to the bottom of the jar.

4

Use a teaspoon to pour the potting mix over the moss.

5

Carefully take a plant and pull it out of its pot and place it into the jar, making sure all the roots are covered with soil.

6

Seal the jar with the lid. The terrarium is done, you do not even need to water the plants as they create moisture which condenses on the jar and back into the roots. Keep the jar in a bright room but out of direct sunlight.

The days are getting warmer now and I can see you've been reading so much, the explorer in you is growing fast, and I can sense a need to wander, farther off. Are you ready for a longer walk, an expedition through the trees? Binoculars are good to have but eyes and ears are all you need.

What will you discover?

The Woods

3

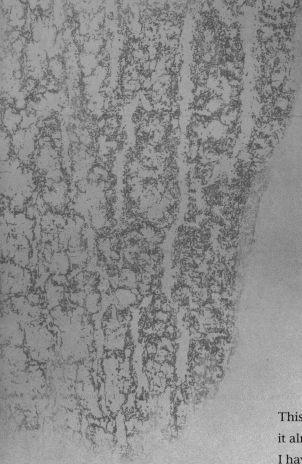

This feels like a giant, my hand fits so well on its bark. I can sense
it almost moving, there's so much beating in its heart! So very tall,
I have to crane my neck to see, little bits of blue sky through
shimmering canopy. The leaves are like maps, somewhere
everyone can go, veins like flowing rivers, this feels like home.

There's an explosion of movement, a cackling cacophony, a flash
of blue wing is landing, right above me. It's moving very quickly,
like a mechanical toy bird. Hopping from branch to branch belting
out a rasping call. Silver crown with black dashes, the pink blush of
chest is so soft. Posture of a queen sat amongst her leafy throne.

How long have we been looking? My neck is getting sore but I'm
so brilliantly happy, shall we explore some more? There is violet
everywhere and a snaked path through the calf-deep waves. Bells
curving, gracefully drooping like the last colour of the rainbow closest
to the earth. The flower tide pulls running feet deeper into the wood.

Noticing. Tree begins to gently pulse and vibrate. Blurred wings.
Sunlit stripes, barely there, flickering among the leaves. Little bodies
bouncing, pecking, scrambling along branches. High-pitched squeak
bubbles and trills from smallest scissor beak. Laughter bellows out of
belly and they're gone, but warmth remains.

FACTS

OAK TREE

It is said that oaks live for 900 years – 300 for growing, 300 for living and 300 for dying. The **OAK TREE** will make 10 million acorns in its lifetime, so it's probably ok to take a few. The oak is the king of the trees in the wood and is very likely to be hit by lightning due to its height above the ground. An oak tree can support over 280 species of insects.

JAY

The Latin name for a JAY is *Garrulus glandarius*. The first part means noisy and chattering, which comes from their cackling call. The second part means 'of acorn' and this comes from their habit of eating mostly acorns and hiding them away to eat later. They often forget where they left them, which spreads the oak trees through the forest. The blue on the jay feathers isn't actually blue but is really a dazzling trick of the light.

BLUEBELL

The sap from the BLUEBELL was used in medieval times to stick the flight feathers onto the arrows used in battles. It is said that the fairies live inside the bells, and that if you hear them ringing it will kill you. It takes five years for a bluebell to grow from a seed to a bulb, which will then produce beautiful flowers. So please treat these flowers with care and do not pick them. Nearly all the different parts of the bluebell are poisonous, which stops creatures eating them.

GOLDCREST

The GOLDCREST weighs only 5 grams, the weight of a twenty-pence coin. It was once believed that goldcrests couldn't make their migration from Scandinavia because they were so small, and that they actually rode on the back of a woodcock. The goldcrest's call is so high-pitched that many older people cannot hear it.

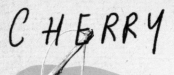

OAK   PINE   CHERRY

TREES
AND THEIR
PROPAGATION

Do you have a favourite tree? There are lots of different types of tree and part of their wonder is how trees and woodland regenerate and create new trees by making a variety of seeds, fruits, berries and nuts.

You must be familiar with the horse chestnut or conker in autumn? Conkers are really just big, beautiful, shiny seeds that in the right conditions can grow into a huge horse chestnut tree. My favourite, the acorn, is a type of nut that grows into the king of trees, the oak. Then there are cherries, which are the delicious fleshy fruits containing a stone or seed which will grow into a cherry tree.

HORSE CHESTNUT   HAZEL   OLIVE

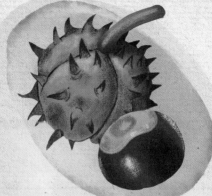

Cherries and conkers develop from delicate spring blossoms, attracting insects with their colours and perfumes. The female parts of the flowers hold eggs that will eventually grow seeds. First they must be pollinated by insects, such as bees and butterflies. Pollen looks like yellow dust and it's the male part of the flower. As insects feed on the delicious sugary nectar inside a flower they pick up pollen on their legs and bodies. When they visit another flower the pollen is transferred to its eggs, and fertilises them. The fertilised eggs then begin to grow into seeds and the female parts of the flower grow into fruits, nuts or berries.

Some trees do not use insects to transfer pollen. Hazel trees produce male catkins at the end of summer which produce pollen that is cast out into the air in spring and carried by the wind. Tiny female red flowers on hazel catch this pollen and over six months develop into a cob or hazelnut. Mighty oaks also use wind to spread their pollen. Both trees create a nut that contains food that helps give a young sapling a head start in growing above other plants in the spring. This food, wrapped up in a tight and hard shell, is also very important for animals and birds that collect them in underground food stores for winter.

Animals, especially birds, enjoy eating fruits and seeds. Often, the seeds pass through the animals' bodies and are pooed out, far from the parent tree.

Other trees, such as sycamore, ash and lime trees, have clever little wings that help them to catch the air and glide and soar to put their roots down in soil far away from their parent tree. Collect them, drop them from a height and watch them spin to the ground!

Are there any other trees and their seeds, berries, nuts and fruit that you can think of?

WHAT IS LIVING ON AN OAK TREE?

YOU WILL NEED:

An oak with branches low enough to shake

A torch

A white sheet

A magnifying glass

1 Stretch the sheet out under the tree. Shake the branches very gently above the sheet to get the insects to fall out of the tree and onto the ground.

2 As the sheet is white it should be easy to spot all the creatures. You can use a magnifying glass to get a closer look. Please be very gentle with all the creatures and, if you can, carefully return them to the leaves and branches.

3 You can also hang up the sheet once it is dark and shine a torch on it. This will attract moths to your garden, and you can spend hours trying to identify them as there are so many of them.

4 You can log your findings in a notebook or on apps like iNaturalist and iRecord.

BLACK ANT

RED UNDERWING
MOTH

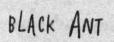

LADYBIRD

MAY BUG

GREEN OAK MOTH

Collect an acorn, plant it, watch
it grow– it will outlive you and
become your legacy to nature.

4

Go i

UPLA

NG
ND

We've come to the end of the forest now, but we still have lots of time. Look at all that space up there, shall we follow the path to sun and sky? Let's feel the air and wind up high. Imagination sparks in us, when the world opens wide. We can breathe more deeply here, let's leave what we know behind.

What can you imagine?

It feels like other beings could live here, shadows amongst the bristly
purple flowers. Bushy protection against the harsh gusts and racing
clouds. Oh, there's the tiniest little creature here, nestled among
the blossom, red-black and spotted, crawling on my finger. Tickly,
feathery legs, parachuting wings are vibrating. Wow, look at it fly!

In the mist a ghost is rising, sparkling with black-tipped wings.
A brown-flecked bird is ascending, joining forces, becoming two.
Tumbling through the air now, circling, scything, sky dancing.
Breath is held in deeply, the world has suddenly stopped, my feet
are rooting in here, a spellbound witness to awe.

Finding it hard to move now, a tear has slipped down my cheek, but a gust of air thrusts a dazzling of wings, and one chooses to land on my bright blue sleeve. Soundless, opening and closing, blazing copper fire, with bright orange patterns, stained-glass light. It rests for but a few seconds before cloud catches it, and the breeze pulls it away. And all is away.

Coming down, racing, as the time has ticked too fast, but we seem to have left the mist behind and gasp! Ascending song is space-bound. Sun-catcher wings paddling the air, never missing a beat. Bubbling notes, defiant strokes, what puppeteer holds you? Suspended, our heart strings plucked as breath-taking love, for all life, spills out. This is living.

Hen Harrier

HEN HARRIERS engage in a beautiful dance in the air, which includes steep climbs, and dives while doing barrel rolls. This display is done by the male to try to entice a female, who also joins in. This behaviour has earned Hen Harriers the nickname of SKYDANCERS. The male gives food to the female on the nest by dropping the food and the female does a backflip to catch it.

WHITE HEATHER is said to be the final resting place of a fairy and a sprig will give a person luck. In Norse mythology the great wolf Fenrir is trapped on an island called Lyngvi, which means 'The Island of Heather'. The white heather burned Fenrir if he put his paw on it. So the wolf was trapped with the help of an enchanted rope called Gleipnir. It can be very wet up on the heath, so bees struggle to pollinate the heather. However, a small insect called a thrip lives inside the bells and does the pollinating instead.

←THRIP

WHITE HEATHER

SKYLARK

The **SKYLARK** is famous for ascending and hovering high in the air, giving one of the most exquisite and complex songs. These displays last for about three to five minutes, but some have been recorded doing the flying orchestra for over thirty. When coming back down again they will always land on the earth, never on tree or bush.

PAINTED LADY

The **PAINTED LADY** butterfly goes on an incredible migration from North Africa. The entire journey cannot be completed in the lifespan of just one butterfly. It takes them six generations. They make the most of strong winds to carry them far and fast, reaching speeds of 45km per hour and travelling up to 160km per day. These amazing voyagers are found in most parts of the world and many types of habitat.

ARCTIC TERN travels from the Arctic to the Antarctic, over 70,000km, beginning its journey in August or September and arriving home again in May or June. They migrate to follow the summer sun as the seasons change.

ARCTIC TERN ⸺ OUTWARD ⸺ RETURN

EUROPEAN
EEL

⸺ OUTWARD
⸺ RETURN

PAUSE

EELS journey from European rivers to the Sargasso Sea, which is about 4,800km some time between August and December. They make this journey as a part of their life cycle, which starts with the eels being spawned in the Sargasso Sea between December and February. Underwater currents take the eels up into the lakes and rivers of Europe where they live most of their lives. Then the currents take them back to the Sargasso Sea to breed and spawn the next generation.

MIGRATION

Do you ever wonder why some creatures only appear at certain times during the year? Animals are brilliant at knowing what is the best environment for them, so they will move huge distances to get to just the right place in order to survive. Isn't nature just incredible?!

WHY DO ANIMALS MIGRATE?

Animals migrate for various reasons. It could be that food will run out in winter, forcing them to move to a place where food is plentiful. Winter may also be too cold for some animals, so if they cannot hibernate, they must travel to a warmer climate. Some creatures, particularly sea creatures, will only give birth at specific places, too.

WHERE DO ANIMALS MIGRATE TO?

Animals can make migrations over vast distances. A common route for many animals is to travel from the Arctic countries down to the warmer African ones, then back again as the seasons change.

WHICH ANIMALS MIGRATE?

All sorts of animals migrate, from the birds you might see in your garden, to eels and whales (even some jellyfish)!

SWALLOWS AND SWIFTS These graceful and swooping birds migrate from Europe to the Southern parts of Africa in winter, which is about 22,000km. They stay in Europe for the summer before heading back to Africa when insect numbers begin to fall.

SWIFTS AND SWALLOWS

— OUTWARD
— RETURN

WHOOPER SWAN

— OUTWARD
— RETURN

WHOOPER SWANS travel from Iceland to the UK in a journey which is about 1,400km long. They arrive in October and stay until spring, because all the nutritious food disappears under the snow and ice during the Arctic winter.

MAKING A
JOURNEY STICK

YOU WILL NEED:

- Anything you can find out in nature, like feathers, flowers and leaves. Make sure that when you pick flowers there are lots of them left and that they are not rare or protected

- Some string or glue

- A stick

1. Go out into the woods or on the heath and collect feathers, flowers and leaves.

2. Remember to be respectful and loving of our natural world and not take too much.

3. Use glue or string to attach them to your stick.

4. Put your journey stick in a place you can see it to remind you of your journeys.

The RIVER

5

We are feeling very breathless, I think we need to cool down. Let's take our shoes and socks off and feel the source of all life. The river beckons you in now, to bring the journey to a close, but I'm sure there are treasures hiding, beneath the gentle flow. Let's slowly put our hands in but keep our eyes open wide, listen too for softer sounds, the banks also hold surprises.

Weaving watery tickles, shadows flicking amongst fingers and toes. Eddying leaves, pushing past, like little boats, with no mast. Eye-catching, glistening after turning stone, oh moving twig and sand shell, where have you come from? Your armour marching slowly, across my silty hand, I think I'll put you back now to roam the riverside.

Pressing hand into pre-made print, I feel the mark you made. One deep hole per fingertip, wondering how you moved. Did you slink or did you trundle, or did you whizz like a burst of light, or maybe you slid under the water, in and out of sight? I feel the warmth of the mud and hope we didn't chase you away. I'll be more careful next time.

A whirring of wings, charged flight, commanding the air like a river knight. Sword like tail directing, dashing, patrolling up and down. What are you searching for, river knight? What do you pursue? Are you hunting for your dinner, looking for somewhere to rest? I hope you find some stillness in some watery, reedy place.

Rainbow flight, flashing past, did I imagine I just saw you? Feathers so sparkling and blinding, beak so sharp, so defining. Who did you bargain with to shine so bright, for you have caught all colours of nature? There you are again now, as real as all the other wings flew, but the day has saved the brightest till last as the sun slipped from the sky. Thank you, dear little river bird, and every living thing that makes our world so special and worth living in.

Our journey has come to a close now and it's time to go back the way we came. Travelling full circle, nature is just the same. Every small thing is connected to you and me, and every other person and creature affect the way we thrive. Hop onto my back now, I can see you are very tired, close your eyes and dream now, let it all go inside.

Tadpoles

The metamorphosis of the FROG is one of the most magical but also most accessible acts of transformation in nature. The cycle starts with an egg in which a black bead begins to grow. When the TADPOLE bursts out it eats the frogspawn it was hatched in and begins to eat the algae and plants in a pond. It gets hungrier and hungrier until it starts to eat insects. It grows bigger and bigger and gets legs. Finally, it loses its gills and uses its lungs instead. Journeying beyond the pond and becoming an adult frog.

'CAMOUFLAGED'

'NAKED'

CADDISFLY LARVAE

CADDISFLY LARVAE are the master camouflage artists of the water bed, covering their little bodies with tiny pebbles, sticks and grains of sand. You can identify caddisfly larvae by the material they choose to go undercover with but some are naked! Caddisfly larvae grow into beautiful adults with wings that look like stained glass windows.

KINGFISHER

KINGFISHERS use their expert eyesight to be able to judge exactly where fish are under the water. They have a sleek body and long beak, which helps when they dive. The long beak is also essential to catch their slippery prey. Once they have caught a fish, they bring it up to a branch. The kingfisher bashes the fish to stun it before eating – nobody wants to eat a wriggling fish.

DIPPER

DIPPERS have a third, transparent eyelid that they can close so they can see under water. They use their wings to force themselves downwards so they don't get carried away with the flow in the river. They have special flaps that cover the nostrils and stop water flooding into the bird's nose.

They are so adapted for river life that their blood can hold extra oxygen, allowing them to hold their breath for thirty seconds.

RIVER OTTER

RIVER OTTERS can hold their breath for up to eight whole minutes, which is longer than their cousins the sea otters, who can only hold it for five. Otters have dense, waterproof fur that keeps them warm, even in icy water. The sea otter has the densest fur of any animal – with up to 125,000 hairs per square centimetre.

The fastest otter in the world is the GIANT RIVER OTTER, which lives in the Amazon and can grow up to 2m long from its wet nose to the tip of its tail.

DRAGONFLIES have nearly 360-degree vision with a small blind spot directly behind the head. Dragonflies are great survivors and amongst Earth's most ancient flying insects. Some of their fossils date from 300 million years ago: long before the dinosaurs. The largest dragonflies have wingspans of 19cm, but their oldest relatives had wingspans of up to 75cm.

DRAGONFLIES

1. EGG

LADYBIRDS

METAMORPHOSIS comes from a Greek word and means shape-changing. Many creatures, especially insects, change dramatically from their hatching form to their adult form. Like a wheel turning, during their life cycle butterflies transform from caterpillars, crawling and eating plants, to a chrysalis – their pupal form – and then to a flying, nectar-drinking adult.

You may well know about BUTTERFLIES but did you know that LADYBIRDS go through a big change too?

2. LARVA

1. In spring the female ladybird lays EGGS on plants which have lots of food on them, such as GREENFLY (APHID). Some are vegetarian and eat mildew (fungus) on plant leaves instead. The eggs are yellow or orange and hatch in about 5–10 days.

2. Hatching ladybird LARVAE are wingless and need to eat so they can form a PUPA. A pupa is an insect in the stage after it has been a larva and before it becomes an adult, during which it is held in and protected by a hard covering and does not move.

3. During the pupal stage they go through metamorphosis and emerge as ladybirds.

4. On emerging from pupa, ladybirds need to feed so they can fly and find a mate. Eggs are laid a few months later.

4. Adult

In autumn, ladybirds gather in large groups under leaves or ivy. Good gardeners leave ivy or create ladybird houses knowing that all their munching of pests like greenfly or cleaning plants of infestations of mildew is such a great help. Ladybirds are a friend to gardeners!

3. PUPA

Metamorphosis

One of nature's most fascinating and magnificent acts of beauty and wonder.

DRAGONFLIES

4. ADULT

DRAGONFLIES

have three distinct stages to their life
cycle with a period of moulting, too.

1. The dragonfly lays eggs on water plants just
below the surface.

2. The emerging young are fierce predators of ponds and streams. Adapted for
underwater life, they have gills and large, extendable jaws to catch and
eat other water creatures, including small fish and tadpoles. They also
have a secret water jet-propulsion trick to quickly get them out
of danger.

3. Unlike many other insects, dragonflies do not have a pupal stage
and change from a larva to their adult form. They spend many years
as larvae, growing bigger and bigger. Finally, they climb up to the water
surface and crawl out into the air. Their skin moults. And...

4. A glorious adult dragonfly has emerged, so unlike their larvae. It will
zoom off to catch insects in the air, becoming the emperor of life above
ponds, rivers and lakes. Mating and egg laying soon follows
and the cycle starts again.

1. Egg

3. Moulting

2. Larva

Metamorphosis also occurs in frogs and toads. Their young also have a water-living
stage, the head resembles a frog or toad, but the body is fish-like, and gills let them
breathe underwater. Emerging from clumps of jelly like eggs or spawn if it's a frog or a
long-beaded string of eggs for a toad. The young develop quickly, growing back legs and then front
legs, the tail shortening and the mouth getting larger. Eventually they become a froglet or toadlet,
ready to leave the water to live and hunt for food on land.

POND DIPPING

EXPLORING RIVERS AND PONDS

YOU WILL NEED:

A net

A tray to put the creatures in

Wellies or water shoes

A river or pond

A grown-up!

1. Please do take care when you go into the water, avoid deep, fast-flowing, wide rivers. Don't go into the water if it is higher than your ankle and always be accompanied by an adult. Your local Rivers Trust can help you.

2. Fill the tray with water from the pond or river.

3. Wade into the shallows of the river and find a good spot with lots of sediment and a water flow that isn't too fast.

4. Kick up into the mud, which will lift all the creatures up into the water.

5. Sweep the net through the water, trying to steer away from plants that can catch on the fabric.

6. Pour the contents into the tray and search for all the little creatures like Daphnia, also known as water fleas, and if you are lucky you might see water boatmen or dragonfly nymphs.

TADPOLES

WATER SNAILS

STICKLEBACK

POND SKATERS

WHIRLIGIGS

CRUCIAN CARP

NEWT

CADDISFLY LARVAE

Hello again
Wild Child

Now that you have begun your journey of discovery, so much more awaits. I have merely shown you a microcosm of what there is to know about nature, a key to a door. Now it's time for you to open it wide. I hope you'll spend many happy hours fuelling your curiosity for the world and the part you play in it.

We are all connected to nature and everything is connected to the web of life, all held together by invisible threads that you can't see but can feel when your knowledge grows. LEARNING ABOUT THE NATURAL WORLD IS REALLY IMPORTANT, it helps us realise who we are, our humanity and our place within it.

We can all connect with our inner wild child. I believe every child is an innate naturalist. That means that we are born into the world wanting to know more and to discover nature. Going for walks with your family, noticing and recording what you see is a brilliant and simple way to become fascinated and knowledgeable about our incredible wildlife, but that is just the beginning. Once you've entered the world of realising your love for our beautiful planet, you'll just want to cherish it and protect it – because NATURE IS FRAGILE, AND IT NEEDS OUR HELP. I just know that you'll want to do everything you can to make a difference.

When out in nature, BE GENTLE AND KIND TO THE PLANTS AND ANIMALS YOU DISCOVER. Pick those sunlit dandelions and daisies and look at them closely, but leave more rare wildflowers, such as bluebells, in the ground. You can read some more about your local area and learn which flowers are abundant and not at risk of low numbers. I always love to look and gently touch plants, take some photos and make memories, rather than picking them. I like to leave them where they love to grow. The outside world is at its most beautiful when we treat it with kindness, leaving no trace that we've ever been there. We should only leave the echoes of our laughter.

When out in nature, **MAKE SURE YOU DRESS FOR THE WEATHER!** If you're going upland, even if it's sunny at the bottom, weather changes dramatically at a height – so never go upland or into the mountains unless you are well prepared with strong boots, lots of layers and snuggly gloves and a hat to keep you warm and safe. Pack it all in a backpack with snacks, water and a map – mobile phone signal can be really patchy in remote areas.

THERE ARE MANY WILDLIFE ORGANISATIONS YOU CAN BECOME INVOLVED WITH. You can do really cool garden wildlife surveys which help scientists: such as the Big Garden Birdwatch, the Big Butterfly Count and the Great British Wildflower Hunt. It's even possible with some of these charities to volunteer your time as a family, or when you're older, you can give your time as a young person and help them protect nature! I volunteer with my local Wildlife Trust and it makes me feel so good to know that I am helping them to raise awareness of the wonderful creatures we share our local area with. There is a list at the back, check them out!

Lastly, have fun, enjoy the journey and the feeling that you are connecting with an ancient part of yourself. Something that you share with all humans on Earth, who have ever lived. You are nature. You are a very important part of something magnificent. Go out into the world and make it better. **I BELIEVE IN YOU.**

Dara

GLOSSARY

Antenna
An animal's feeler that can be used to sense touch, and sometimes taste and smell, too. Most insects have two antennae.

Bulb
A round part of a plant that grows underground and stores food over winter. Plants that have bulbs are often the first ones to flower in spring.

Catkin
A flower spike that hangs from wind-pollinated trees such as willow and hazel.

Classification
A system used by scientists to organise living things into groups, by similarities or by the way they evolved and are related to each other.

Continent
A very large area of land, such as Africa, Europe or Asia.

Dimorphism
When the male and female animals of one species look very different to each other.

Evolved
Animals and plants that have evolved have changed over time, to survive in an ever-changing world.

Fertilisation
When pollen, which is a male part of a flower, joins with a female part (an egg). A fertilised egg can then grow into a seed.

Gills
The breathing organs used by many animals that live in water, such as fish, crustaceans and some insects.

Insect
An animal that has three pairs of legs and a body that is divided into three main parts: head, thorax and abdomen.

Larva
The soft-bodied young of some animals, such as insects. Caterpillars and fly maggots are both types of larvae.

Lungs
The breathing organs used by many animals that live in air.

Mandible
A jaw.

Metamorphosis
The change in body shape that takes place when some types of animal grow into adults.

Microcosm
A collection of living things, a place or a system that is very small but which works in the same way as a much larger collection, place or system.

Migration
A journey that animals go on to find resources, such as food or water.

Moult
When animals, such as insects or crustaceans, shed their old skin so they can grow bigger.

Nectar
A sugary liquid made by flowers to attract animals, especially insects, to visit them.

Nymph
The growing phase of an insect before metamorphosis.

Organism
A living thing, such as an animal, fungus or plant.

Pollination
When pollen is transferred from the male part of a flower to a female part of a flower.

Pollinator
An animal, such as an insect, bat or bird, that transfers pollen between flowers.

Predator
An animal that hunts other animals to eat.

Propagation
The process of growing new plants, often from seeds.

Pupa
The stage in an insect's life cycle when it is undergoing metamorphosis and changing from its larval form to its adult form.

Species
Groups of similar organisms which can produce fertile offspring.

Terrarium
A glass container, which is usually sealed, in which plants are grown.

HELPFUL ORGANISATIONS

Bat conservation trust www.bats.org.uk

BTO – British Trust for Ornithology www.bto.org

Bumblebee Conservation Trust
www.bumblebeeconservation.org

Butterfly Conservation www.butterfly-conservation.org

Jane Goodall Institute www.janegoodall.org

Marine Conservation Society www.mcsuk.org

National Trust www.nationaltrust.org.uk

National Trust for Scotland www.nts.org.uk

Buglife www.buglife.org.uk

The Rivers Trust www.theriverstrust.org

RSPB – Royal Society for the Protection of Birds
www.rspb.org.uk

The Wildlife Trusts
www.wildlifetrusts.org

Wildlife Watch
www.wildlifewatch.org.uk

DARA McANULTY is an award-winning author, naturalist and activist from Northern Ireland. He's received many awards for his conservation work, including from BBC *Springwatch*, *The Daily Mirror* and *Birdwatch* magazine. Dara is the youngest ever recipient of the RSPB medal for conservation. He lives with his family and Rosie the rescue greyhound at the foot of the Mourne Mountains in County Down. His first book *Diary of a Young Naturalist* won the 2020 Wainwright Prize for Nature Writing, the An Post Irish Book Award for Newcomer of the Year 2020, the Books Are My Bag Readers Award for Non-Fiction 2020 and was shortlisted for the Waterstones Book of the Year.

BARRY FALLS grew up in rural Northern Ireland, where he spent a lot of time drawing pictures and writing stories to go with them. He is a commercial illustrator, who has received multiple awards for his work with clients such as *The New York Times*, *American Airlines* and *The Telegraph*.